A

Book

ABOUT

Us

A Book

ABOUT

Us

A HEART'S CONTINUING JOURNEY TO LOVE

TONIO

I-Am Love
Publications

I-Am Love Publications

ISBN-10: 0692918175

ISBN-13: 978-0692918173

This one is for us.

Contents

And to think that day, had you not smiled, I would have never known your name, and you wouldn't have stolen my heart.

To the most beautiful person in my world:

My days are forever bright with every sight of you. And perhaps you are yet to understand what it is exactly that I see in you. But I love watching how you maneuver your way into and around my heart, as if you've always lived there…as if you're home.

Because of you, it's real...

Some people don't believe in God. I'm aware of that, but I don't care what others believe, except that I can't write this book without thanking Him for everything. For you, for me, for us. Without His blessing and saving grace I wouldn't have met *you* when I did. The way I did. And though none of this has been the swiftest journey, I look back at everything—the good and bad moments—and smile at the lesson we learned in order to arrive here in a place in our hearts, a place in our lives called 'us.'

Let us continue the Journey to Love.

On Emotional Maturity

I've matured. It's obvious in my way of thinking, and most certainly in my beliefs. Somehow the way I used to love was somewhat selfish, and perhaps that's how it is for many people like myself who were taught to be a certain way. I didn't exactly have a *love* figure in my life in a way I could mirror, except for some scripted love stories. Not to say there's something wrong with a scripted love story, but you cannot compare your reality with what you see on screen. You must love what is and who is with you. Nothing is ever as simple as it may seem. I've met people who have been terrified to tell me they love me for fear of rejection—and, truth be told, I was that person once.

I've loved, and I love truly to this day, but I remember the horrors of searching aimlessly for the right combination of words to express it. I was afraid of sounding a certain way or coming off as 'too needy'—and that's natural for first-time lovers and those who find themselves in the lucky situation of being able to experience the magic of love.

I'll confess that some days I have no clue who this new 'me' is, but I like him—because being vulnerable has blessed me with the greatest of friendships and the best of love. This is a complete opposite of who I used to be—the person whom I was taught to be in order to survive in the game.

And that was another mindset I needed to overcome. Love isn't a game. It never was, and it isn't about winning or losing. Be who you are and give of yourself honestly and freely without second-guessing or overthinking the situation.

But love is patience, communication, and, most of all, letting your guard down so you're vulnerable enough to be seen. Vulnerability will beautify you in unimaginable ways. Don't shy away from your truth or give in to pretenses just because you think someone will like you better a certain way.

I've witnessed horrific love stories and betrayal. I've seen big and small scars and people who walk around extremely uncomfortable trying to cover them up. I only wish they wouldn't, so more people could understand their story and see that they are among survivors, soldiers in the war of love.

My friends, healing your wounds takes time. You can't rush the natural process. I know firsthand how painful and unbearable it becomes, even when time has passed, and you're supposed to have felt better by now and you don't. Emotional scars require love and attention to begin healing. Part of this entails forgiveness of both yourself and those who have wronged you. And, as much as you may hate to have to read this, *you are not yet ready to date after a heartbreak.* You cannot simply apply a Band-Aid as if it were a superficial wound and go out there. You'll only begin to bleed again, because almost everything will be a reminder of the past you haven't yet gotten over—and you'll likely hurt someone else in the process who is ready to be with you.

I hope you will enjoy reading this next chapter in my and your continuing journey to love. I also hope that, with every new moment, every new day, we go a step closer to that destination of love everlasting.

The Day We First Met

It was some time ago,
The day we first met,
And I remember thinking,
'How in the world?'
Because I couldn't get myself
To stop smiling at you
As if suddenly I'd been made to know
What happy feels like.
I figured then, that someday,
You and I would be 'us.'

Though It's Soon

I feel like writing.
My lips keep moving incessantly
With every thought,
Feeling so beautiful,
So alive,
Imagining all of the possibilities between us.
I can't explain this sudden attraction,
Stronger than my will to hold back.
But I think of you smiling.
I think of us as if—
Even though it's soon,
Too soon, but love is strange like that—
Arriving unexpectedly.
I can't quite explain yet,
But I want more.
I'm interested in knowing everything.
I want you,
Regardless of what else remains unknown.
For once I want to let go and love,
Live in the moment that is us.

On Respect

In case you were wondering, yes, it's rude to be on your phone or constantly checking it while on a date. I don't care how important you think you are or what business you're taking care of; it can wait!

If someone is on a date with you and disrespecting you as such, then know that they don't value your time or presence and would much rather be elsewhere than in that moment with you.

Now many may disagree and find an excuse for why they need to be on their phones—but that's something we've all become good at: finding excuses for our bad behavior. However, this is one of the many signs you shouldn't ignore. Some signs people give us are subtle, while others are obvious. In this particular scenario, it's the latter. Don't be surprised once you have chosen this person and you come to realize she or he spends more time on the phone than with you.

Which brings me to another situation. I'm well aware of the society and culture we live in where, if there isn't a picture or video, then it didn't happen. So we must constantly point and shoot our camera phones at just about every single thing we do: a pedicure, a kiss, a drive, the foods we eat. Heck, we're even taking social media into our bedrooms—a place of intimacy. I say all this not to judge but to honestly make us think: What are we becoming as humanity?

Every day we are giving up more and more of our privacy, becoming less and less intimate with one another, to a point where we can't look each other in the eyes when we speak all for the sake of public spectacle.

I don't mind sharing happy moments and achievements with friends and family on social media, because, the reality is, we can't all be at the same place at the same time. But we must always think about what we're posting and why we're doing it.

I'd venture to say, some people want to be celebrated, while others want to cause envy among their friends and followers. But that is honestly not the way to go about your life, your existence. Do things with good intentions. Strive to help others, not make them feel less worthy. Celebrate your love, your relationship, and the person you're with. Once you do this, you will realize how amazing your relationship becomes. It's all about focus and intent. Be each other's biggest fans. Honor what you have together.

Something Extraordinary

You'll have options, and
There will be lovers holding out their hands,
But once you've discovered that special feeling...
Nurture it.
Never-mind all the outside noisemakers.
No love story is ever written to perfection.
However, the feeling should always remain:
Something extraordinary.

Sound of Love

Every time we talk,
There's a burning desire for more.
Everything about you is engaging.
If not your eyes, it's your smile—
And let's not talk about the sound of your voice.
It is everything that is beautiful
And I smile every time
Just because it is that joyful sound my spirit adores.

On True Love

It baffles me how many people would continue searching an entire lifetime for something they already have in front of them, ever misguided by historic failures of relationships passed, as well as a culture in which love is a *temporary engagement* of possibilities, built on nothing but superficial reasoning.

Love is indefinite and indefinable, such that most have been taught to fear it, because it's unknown, while others were never taught how to identify it. Hence many are blindly walking around in circles, hoping for something different each time when true love is about delving deeper, uncovering the ugly parts we don't necessarily like about one another, finding beauty in that imperfect nature, and loving it anyway.

The Walk

I took the step you couldn't,
Knowing eternity awaits,
Ready and willing to fight,
But that wasn't necessary—
The magic was still there.
And so, I joined you in the walk
Alongside the waters that flowed freely
Like our love.
It was the first time my steps were firm,
Walking confidently in the same direction,
Moving past,
Moving forward,
Building a new path
That was us.
This was love.

You were always so evasive, like the moon,
And just when I would think we're getting closer,
I'd realize you're still so far away.

Regret

This morning finds me in a place of utter regret,
Somewhat confused about how or why I'm here,
Having had all of the opportunities
To love and be loved
As I've always dreamed.
But instead I chose to play victim
Of my circumstance, whereby I chose you,
Fearful to try, only to end up feeling
Like such a fool,
Unable to exit this hell
Where my days are spent
Pretending not to feel
The tears that escape my eyes,
Knowing I made the biggest mistake
The moment I chose familiarity over love.

It's unfair to say,
But I always knew I'd break your heart,
Because the most important pieces of my heart
Still belonged to someone else.

Our Last Fight

Tonight I had to fight
The toughest battle against
Vicious tears
Drowning my sorrows,
Suffocating my heart,
Tearing me apart.
Missing you
Is excruciatingly painful,
And I can't seem to forgive myself,
Not knowing our last fight
Would be our last.

Heart on a Leash

Tethered to an empty promise,
Aware, but hopeful I'll win your love,
While you have my heart
Right where you wanted it—
At bay, docile and obedient,
Responsive to my master's every command
Like the dog I've become,
Tied to a leash of words
Meant to keep me around,
Feeding on every lie.
Some days you play with me,
Other times you don't,
But I still love you
And lick your face and feet,
Wagging my tail in excitement
When you arrive home,
Pulling every trick I know
In attempts to please you.
But it's of no use.
I'm not your best friend—
Or the one you love.

On Abuse

You may have gotten the number,
Perhaps a few dates here and there,
Or even a kiss.
You may have gone as far as the bedroom
But until you have someone's heart,
You have nothing.

The most powerful person in the world is the one holding the key to your heart. Love unlocks doors and creates endless possibilities and opportunities. Yet there is only one key to the heart, and that is *genuine love*—no duplicates or manufacturing of any kind.

And it goes without saying that the very same person who loves us has the potential to destroy us. Some people use love to destruct and mistreat us. Understand that just because we love someone does *not* give that person the right to abuse and misuse us. We have the choice of saying no and putting an end to it all.

Don't ever allow anyone to hide behind love and use it as a weapon of destruction. Anyone can claim they love us, but in the end it's up to us what type of love we choose to accept.

The Nightmare in My Heart

Perhaps it's the stillness of the night
That makes me uneasy,
Or my relentless pursuit
Of a heart I cannot attain.
But again,
It's all just questions unanswered,
While you clearly couldn't care less about the horrors
Of my heart's nightmare.

Hiding My Heart

I never show the world
Just how broken my heart is.
It's easier to hide it than having to explain
Why it looks the way it does—
Bruised and badly injured beyond recognition.
And people like me are misjudged,
Made out to be *'undesirable goods'* in the market,
Where it's cooler to shy away from emotions
Than to show them,
Because dealing with one's feelings is a 'drag.'
Sadly, I've succumbed to this norm of existence
Where I fake a smile
And respond with rehearsed lines
That leave little to no room for explanation
Or the start of a conversation.

Liquid Courage

We spend lonely nights hugged to a bottle
Hoping it would give us courage to speak the truth of what's on our minds—but we end up feeling just as empty as the bottles we drink from— and in the same uncomfortable bed and position where we fuck until we come to the conclusion that what we have is just that— mindless sex and a loveless relationship.

Desperation

Sometimes desperation can rationalize absurdity
And make us accept late nights with people
Who don't care to see the color of our eyes,
Let alone know our name.
It isn't our place to judge, nor should we ever—
And sometimes we are just ignorant
Because we have not been taught—
But we're so much more—
And we deserve someone to look into our eyes
And know our name.
Just remember that.

I just wish I knew sooner
Before falling asleep
And dreaming of us.

Losing You, Loving You

I still get scared at the thought
Of ever losing you.
I've not gotten comfortable
Or taken anything we have for granted.
My heart still smiles every time we meet,
Every time you're near,
And every day I'm blessed to call you mine.
I love you
Because there's a peace you bring to my heart
That I've not been able to find anywhere
Or with anyone else
But you.

My Beautiful Everything

I love that you're stunning
Without being arrogant—
A welcoming blessing
To everyone who experiences your smile
In your effortless way
Of making others feel valued.
And I am the luckiest person
Who gets to call you
My beautiful everything.
And I can't thank you enough
For gracing me with all that is you.

On Self-Love

It's an inside job that only you can get done. No amount of likes, comments and compliments will ever cause you to love yourself.

Self-love is not a Band-Aid term we should use to cover up the real hurt we feel inside. Most important, self-love isn't a nicely done selfie we pose for and post on the gram. Self-love, my friends, is much deeper than that. It is showcased in the types of things we tolerate from people, whether in relationships or life in general. It's the ambition and fire we have inside that pushes us to go hard and do better for ourselves no matter what, because we *know* we deserve just that. Self-love is ultimately a healing compound—and it should be applied liberally to all of our wounds.

Take this from someone who practically had to reinvent himself. Most of who I am today came as result of many years of struggling to discover my greatness. You see, many times we feel there is something special about us, deep inside—and there is. But the people around us can sometimes influence how negatively or positively we view ourselves.

Growing up, I had these kinds of individuals in my life. Worse yet, they were family—people I trusted as a child to love and care for me, and instead they did the opposite and broke me down to a point where I felt utterly insignificant.

It's not important that I name them or get too specific at this stage in my life, because this story is not about them. It's not about the people who cause us pain, but more about us—the individuals who overcome tragedies and fight the toughest battles every single day to come out on top.

Looking back, I suppose they didn't know how badly their words affected me then. But they did in so many ways, to the point where I turned to food as a way to fill whatever was missing on the inside.

It wasn't until many years later, as an adult, that I would realize that love was the single most important factor missing in my life. It was the void I had been so desperately attempting to fill with food, late nights, to no avail. More important, I finally understood that no amount of consumption or seclusion would ever suffice, because what I needed to do was to feed my soul with love, not my body with more food.

I'll be brutally honest: Falling in love with yourself is no easy process. It's hard. It almost feels as if your mind, body, and spirit are separate entities at war with each other, where hate always seems to win, subsequently causing one to surrender to depression and self-loathing.

In this situation, I found that self-talk was crucial to my rehab. During this process, I did a lot of negotiation among the different parts of me. I had to convince myself that all of those hurtful words were lies told to me because I was someone to be feared, something extraordinary beyond their reason, hence their victim. But through the process, the saddest, most heartbreaking step was unlearning self-hatred. And that's a story requiring much detail, due to its complexity.

Nevertheless, here I am now—an author of love, a man of imperfections yet extraordinary in every way. And the most beautiful part of it all is, I won't ever allow anyone to make me believe otherwise, nor should you. Ever.

Some days I look back and thank my family for making my upbringing difficult, because without the role they played I probably wouldn't be the strong person I am today.

At times I'm someone whose smile can mislead you to think I don't hurt. But I've learned that the strongest people aren't the ones who continue to fake smiles. They are those who let out the tears.

So love yourself enough to expose your soul. Share your pain and hurt, because covering up how we feel only leads us further into exclusion where people don't see us the way they should. They begin to put us in a category of "unrelatable" when the reality is, we all hurt, and pain has a uniting force if people allow themselves the opportunity to show real emotions.

On Finding Ourselves

Maybe the answer isn't to find someone else, but to find yourself.

Most of us are under the false impression that we need another person in our lives to feel complete or to move on from a heartbreak—but that isn't the case. Healing from emotional wounds takes time and lots of self-care and love. So it's important to have honest conversations with yourself about what happened and why, and to quit pointing fingers and blaming everyone else; that won't solve anything, and it surely won't bring the love back.

Take this opportunity to spoil yourself and rekindle an important relationship that is often broken when people get into romantic relationships. They forget who they are and how amazing they can be when alone. Once you've rebuilt a strong bond between your mind, spirit and soul, you are ready to go back out there and meet new people. The most important thing to remember is to be *honest* with yourself, no matter how painful the truth may be. Honesty is the best and only way to begin the healing process.

Be crazy about yourself.

Somehow we think it's wrong and shunned upon to be utterly in love with ourselves. Yet nothing happens without self-love. I don't mean this in a narcissistic kind of way, but what's wrong with admiring our talents and abilities and appreciating our flaws and imperfections? What's wrong with reassuring ourselves that we matter, that we're good and worthy of all of the best? I believe that the moment we all start to realize that life is much more than our outward appearance, we begin to truly understand the beauty of love.

Here's the thing. You're absolutely amazing, no matter what anybody else thinks. So stop doubting yourself. And, despite the scars and flaws, you are worth everything good in this lifetime, including love.

I understand that some of us believe our worthiness of love depends only on how well we lead our lives or how 'morally pure' we are, but that's not true. All of our journeys are and will continue to be different. Some of us will have a tougher life than others—but, no matter where life takes us, we are still capable of loving again and again. If you've been cheated on before, don't think you deserved it as an excuse to continue to allow such blatant disrespect for yourself.

Finally, our body weight and shape do not determine our worthiness of love! So make an effort to find yourself and cultivate better self-love.

We keep killing ourselves trying to appeal and please the wrong people. Going to the extreme sometimes, just so that someone may notice or love us and that's absurd. Yes, we may have a quirky side or something different that we do, that's not widely accepted—but who cares?!? As long as we learn to love what makes us unique, other people's opinions don't matter.

Don't be that fool that — changes his or herself to a point beyond recognition. That's how we lose sight of ourselves. I genuinely believe we're all made perfect in His image — based on his plans for us. Anyone who's meant to love us, will. Regardless of how 'weird' or 'messy' we may seem to the rest of the world. Again, there is nothing wrong with you. Stop stressing trying to fix what doesn't need fixing. Self-improvement and development is not the same as a 'fix.' Remember that, because you'll always be perfect in the eyes of the one meant to see you.

Havoc

An awkward silence now havocs my soul
While seeking a peace I can't seem to find.
And though you've given me the truth,
It's just so unsettling.
I can't comprehend this new reality,
Thinking I knew you well—
When I didn't.

Mediocrity

Sometimes we want to go back to familiarity,
Too frightened of the unknown,
Too afraid to dream…
So we fall asleep in the comforts of mediocrity
Only to wake up in the horror of our reality.

Some people just have an egotistical approach to love
Whereby pride is all consuming,
Ruining every possibility
Of love blossoming fully.

Crime Scene

It's sad how all the places
We've ever been together
Now feel like a crime scene,
Taped off with invisible lines of caution,
and I'm terrified that, if I trespass,
The memories alone
Can attack with such force
And kill what's left of me.

I know this is crazy,
Because we just met,
But every minute
You're away from me
Is uncomfortable.

Without You

It's hard to be upset
When you look at me that way.
It's difficult to shy away from love
When it has your face and your name,
But above all,
It's impossible to imagine a single moment
Without you in my life.

You are the best of all my friends,
The most beautiful among all flowers,
And I love you like never before in my life.
I hope that, whenever you feel like crying
You'll remember that I am one who adores you.

On Communication

The reality is always somewhat different
From our perception,
Presumably because it's easier
To not face the truth,
Question those we love
Simply because we're afraid of hearing something
Contrary to what we believe.
And I suppose this was one of my many mistakes
When it came to loving you.
I was afraid to ask
All of the important questions.
I wanted to keep seeing you
In the same fluorescent light,
When in actuality there was a dark secret
Holding you back from being mine
The way we were meant to be.

I say all this to say,
Talk and communicate with one another
No matter how difficult it may be
To find the right words.
I've learned that the right combination of words
Doesn't necessarily exist
When it comes to speaking from the heart.
Just let it pour.

Know that, regardless of what's said,
It's important that you don't judge one another,
That you keep an open mind
And remember your love.
Remember love in the times of uncertainty,
And I promise you
You will get through it.

For All Eternity

Tonight we spoke like never before.
I understood your fear,
Even though I promise
I'll never leave your side.
I heard the inflection of pain in your voice
As you muttered those words,
And just as quickly, I responded,
'I'd never trade you for anyone.'
It was my most absolute beautiful truth,
And I felt a single tear escape my eyes
Because I was free.
Finally you heard me.
I am yours for all eternity.

Love Like This

Pain too strong
To a point of crippling demise,
But I must face the truth,
Deal with the reality
Of knowing my perception of you was false,
And while loving you the way I do,
You'd been in a situation all along
With someone else
Who I can bet will never love you
With the same maturity, certainty and sincerity
As I ever will.
Just wish I knew the truth
Regardless of how painful it may have been,
And I didn't.

The Ultimate Weapon

This is by far
One of the most heartbreaking chapters,
But it must be written nonetheless,
Regardless of the pain in my heart
And the numbness in my fingers.
It's severe how deep
It all runs through my veins,
Every truth
Unmistakably shaking me to my core,
Every word you say
Cutting into me like a thousand knives
Violently piercing through my skin,
And still I'm just as much in love with you
As I was before knowing you lied.
Agonizing as it may all be,
I keep begging for more truth.
I wanted to know the real you
No matter how bad it was,
And it's interesting to see
How the old part of me
Didn't encourage me to run
When normally I would.
Instead, I was there by your side,
Feeling confused,
Perhaps even abused,

But I forgave it all in that moment
Because I wanted to make us work.
I wanted to spend my life with you
No matter the obstacle.
For the first time
I was a willing soldier for a love war
Because I knew with certainty
I had the ultimate weapon:
Your heart.

Hard Pill to Swallow

The truth is such a hard pill swallow.
And I'm afraid I'll choke
Trying to get a million questions asked
Before you shut down on me again.
I hear every word you're saying,
And yet I cannot comprehend.
I cannot believe I was so blind to the truth.
And suppose I'm to blame
Having allowed myself to become complacent
To a point where I wouldn't dare question
Your whereabouts and your doings.
My mistake.

On Unconstrained Love

Love me loudly. Don't tone it down.

In recent times we've been led to believe that if you love too soon or too strongly it's weird and 'creepy,' that we shouldn't say certain things until some time has passed or else we would scare someone off. But, again, that's society trying to control how we love. That's people promoting their agenda for sexual misconduct and immorality. The less love we see in the media and around us, the easier it is for us to believe that love is something impossible to attain, or something of a fairytale. And that's not so. Love me loudly. If your feelings are true—show it proudly, without constraints or limits, and you'll see how beautifully you'll feel and make the other person feel. And it may be that some people are not receptive to your love. That's okay! But don't you ever stop believing or loving.

Love & Replacements

For me, it was never about doing
Or finding someone 'better.'
That is nothing but a sad mentality
Of the egotistical and superficial.
But I get it.
When the weak can't fight, they run.

I, however, never sought to replace you
Or your memory, despite the appeal of newness.
In fact, leaving you was never an option to begin,
Because I loved you regardless of your flaws,
Beyond your lies and secrets.
I just expected in return
Someone loyal and aggressive,
Able to speak openly and confidently
Despite any of my oppositions.
You were neither,
And I'm beginning to feel like a fool,
Devalued and disrespected.

The Extra

I can neither blame you
Nor hide the upset of it all.
And I suppose I should have known better,
Perhaps should had been stronger
And resisted all of your kisses
As they lured me back in,
But I didn't do so.
I blame myself
For being too stupid to realize
That I was but an extra
In your well-directed romantic drama.

Unfair Dreams

For so long I dreamt
Of waking up with you beside me,
Kissing you good morning
Instead of texting you,
But I understand now that,
Although I love you enough to keep waiting,
It's unfair to keep lying to my heart
That someday you'll choose me
When clearly you belong to someone else
You don't want to hurt.

Resignation

He can have you.
I've decided it's time I let you go,
Because it's not worth
Another sleepless night.
It's not worth my sanity
Having to question from here on
Everything you say
And everything you do.
He can have you.
Because the way I love,
No one else can.
And perhaps it's taken me a long time
To get to this point,
But someday you'll realize
You had a good thing,
Except it will be too late
Because I've chosen to respect myself
And will no longer let you continue
To dehumanize me.

Unforgiving Tears

These tears are just unforgivable today,
Rolling down unannounced
And without mercy,
Reminding me that I can't ignore
The turmoil inside.
And so I wipe them away
Incessantly with my bare hands
Before anyone can see them,
Before they burn a scar onto my cheeks.

The Disillusionment

I drove by your house this morning again,
Hoping and praying I'd see your car out front
And confirm that you have in fact
Been telling the truth.
It was my last hopeful attempt to save my heart
From the disillusionment that would soon come.
And once again…you lied.

Love in the Now

Someday I'll be gone,
And perhaps you'll still be with him,
I don't know.
But I intend on loving you
For as long as I can,
Because I don't believe in tomorrow.
I wouldn't have written our story like this,
Because it's been more painful
Than beautiful at times,
But my love for you
Is what keeps me around.
I'll go to war for you if I must,
And I wouldn't think twice about it
Because I loved you the moment we met,
Knowing absolutely nothing else about you
But that.

Most people don't understand my story.
They don't get why I choose you,
Even though I have options,
And for me it has never been about that—
It has always been about the peace I feel
When I'm with you—
The authentic smile you bring to my face
And the intensity with which my heart beats

When I'm with you.

We've come so far and grown so much.
And, heck, you love differently,
Hardly ever saying much,
But I stuck around
Because my heart wouldn't let me go
Anywhere else that wasn't you.

Made to Order

This is not meant to be an attack on modern dating,
But a mere reflection on what's happening.
We're told to date often
And date multiple people at a time
Until we find 'the right one,'
And the right one only so happens to be
Someone who checks off on a long list
Of 'must be' and 'must have'
As if in love we're meant to pick and choose.
And therein lies the problem,
Because love has somehow become
Like something we manufacture
Based on requisites and specifications.
We forget that we are people, and we all feel.
In a way we become desensitized
To each other's feelings,
Because now love is not about the other person:
It's a selfish endeavor for what we can get
With immediacy, not consistency.

Heartbreaking Sacrifice

It broke my heart to hear you've settled
Somewhere between familiarity and fear
Alongside someone you deem 'not that bad'
When I love you so much.
And I wish I could help you see
Just how wonderful you are,
How fortunate anyone would be to have you.
But your fear weighs more than my love,
So I've accepted to love you from afar
Until I can no more
And hope with all my heart
That somewhere between now and forever
You'll remember the love I showed you
And smile, knowing that even though
You didn't choose me,
I always chose you.

I could hear you talk all day and all night.
Explain to me again and again
How you make that special recipe I love so much.
I don't care, as long as we never stop talking.

Better Left Unsaid

I'll bite my tongue
The next time I want to say
'I love you.'
I'll swallow my every desire
Until I choke, knowing
It's better left unsaid.
I'm at war with words
That feed your ego
While I starve for your love
In agony.

It's Complicated

'It's complicated' is a common status
Found among daters in a world of social media.
These individuals aren't datable, but relatable—
To me and so many others alike,
Stuck in a standstill,
Waiting for someone we love to make the decision
To accept us as a thing, as an item,
And this day often time never comes.
We're attached emotionally and physically,
And for whatever reason we can't untie the knot.
We can't seem to let our grip slip,
So we play a game of chase
And wait while, in all honesty,
That person we love is out there
Living life and exploring all avenues,
And sometimes they come home
Or send a text saying 'I miss you,'
And we fall for it,
Thinking this time things will be different,
But it never quite ends like that.
We're used for sex and company in a time of need
But just as quickly tossed aside
Until we're in demand once again.
I get it.
But at some point we need to respect who we are

And kick them to the curb and not look back.
Because if we don't, soon enough
We'll spend a lifetime of regret
Looking back and wondering where time went,
Why didn't that love arrive,
And the answer is, we were too busy acting a fool
And playing a role of tolerance
Instead of being loved.
Love is not that complicated.

There aren't too many people
Who can hold an effortlessly exciting conversation,
Just as there aren't many people
With whom you automatically connect
Without having to try.
But if and when you do,
Cherish that connection.
It doesn't happen often.

Empty Seat

I'll never get used to the empty passenger side,
Placing my cold hands right there
Where you sat so many times beside me,
Smiling in all your glory.
I miss you every time with all that I am
While driving alone in a circle of uncertainty,
Unsure of where you are now
Or with whom you're riding,
And if you glance over at them
The same way you did me.

When I Cry

And maybe we
Don't deserve each other.
This can't be normal,
Fighting just to make up
Because we love pain.
So every blow is low,
And I let you hit me
Where it hurts most,
Because when I cry
That's when you love me best.

Why I Cry

I cry
Because I know
You no longer love me the same.
You won't say so,
But I feel it in the way
Your eyes avoid me
And the subtlety with which
Your lips reject me.

One-sided Love

There's not one moment
When I'm not thinking of you
And wishing I didn't hear
Those hurtful things you said,
Because, regardless of my forgiveness,
I can't seem to make it less painful,
And what's most upsetting
Is that you have yet to apologize
And somehow have managed
To diminish your infidelity
Into a simple 'mistake,'
One of which I have to live with
Because I forgot
I was the only one who loved.

On Insincerity

I swear you loved me because you said it all the time,
But I learned the hard way that that wasn't the case.

It turns out that the message of the person who says 'I love you' more frequently doesn't necessarily translate into real love. Sometimes it's a ploy to get what they want from a relationship with us. We've got to start demanding a little more than just words as proof of love.

So take note of who's doing all the giving and receiving. Sometimes that's where the answers lie.

When we love one another truly, we find joy in doing nice things for each other without being told or asked. We become thoughtful in that sense.

On What's Inside of Us

We can't help who we fall for, but when we do, we should choose the one who sees the abstract parts of us.

It's easy for people to claim they love us when we look good or have ourselves and our stuff together. It is also easy for us to fall for all of their compliments and praise while quickly forgetting that what really matters is what's on the inside of us—the parts that aren't easily seen or touched, the heart of us, our soul and spirit.

You'll always stop and pay attention when someone comes along and describes you in such a way that you can't recognize it's yourself they are speaking of, because they've been able to capture a side of your soul that is rare and purposefully hidden for that one special person with special eyes who is only meant to *see* you.

Lies and Promises

Some nights I can't sleep,
Feeling your heart vibrate with anxiety
Because you're afraid I'll leave
At any moment.
And you won't say a word,
Because I sealed the promise with a kiss,
But your heart, it knows I'm lying
And planning yet another exit strategy.

TONIO

It's best we leave now,
Badly bruised
Rather than terribly wounded.
We can recover
And hopefully see each other again,
Differently but definitely.

Convenient Reach

And it's not that I would ever want to leave
Because my love is real,
But I just don't know where I belong.
Am I at your side,
Or simply in the distance
Far enough where you can reach me
When it's at your convenience?

Open Relationship

He'll never love you
The way I love you,
Without expectations,
All hours of the day
And without end.

You say you love me
And that you're mine,
But it never feels like so.
I mean, love is uncomfortable at times.
In your face and intense,
Most people can't handle it,
But perhaps there's an inexplicable bond
Between you two
That I can't understand.

So I'll go.

You're romantic without flowers,
Beautiful without makeup.
It's all in the way you move
Gracefully about my heart.

The One and Only

You're still the one
That makes me feel almighty,
Still the one that provokes
My most sincere of smiles.
And while you left
Without a proper goodbye,
You remain the one and only
Whom I love without end.

On the Ring

The ring means nothing
If your spouse is not engaged to your heart.
Commitment is much more than a superficial gift.

True love does not come with a price tag. I know our society tends to make us believe that gifts equate love, that the more we spend on someone, the more it 'proves' our love. But, honestly, how absurd is that? Our soul doesn't crave money. It craves love. Gifts are mere gestures. Never put your heart up for sale, because the person thinking she or he can buy it clearly doesn't see that your heart is *priceless*.

Losing You, Missing You

It feels like I'm losing you,
Slipping away from my heart and life
As if there's no more love
To hold you in place.
And maybe I'm wrong
Or just obsessive
When it comes to us,
But I just miss you
When you're not the same.

A Moment in Time

Not quite sure yet what that was—
A blessing, yes, in so many ways
To have met you when I did,
Helping me survive
Through the darkness
Of yesterday's storms.
But you weren't for me,
And I wasn't for you,
And I know that now,
Well enough to understand
That people have different purposes,
And yours wasn't to love me for eternity
But for a moment in time
Most appropriate for my soul's growth,
But not its eternal bliss.

On Sex

It took yet another morning of waking up next to you to know with certainty that which I already suspected: I don't love you, and you're not the one.

Our relationship was purely sexual with the occasional 'I love you' said to satisfy that other part of me starving for something more.

We're more than just sexual beings. Our souls crave a certain type of intimacy that doesn't happen only in the bedroom. Part of truly knowing love is understanding that it is more than sex: is your partner attentive to your emotional needs as well? Does your partner make you feel as though you're the most beautiful person in the world, because, in all respects, you are?

Crying of My Soul

I was stupid once,
Sharing my body with strangers
Wanting to get off,
Hoping it would fill
Whatever void I was experiencing,
Not realizing how damaging
Every encounter was to my spirit.
And it wasn't so much about the emptiness
That soon followed the act,
But rather the uncomfortable
Crying of my soul.

After the Honeymoon Phase

We stopped being intimate
Having more fights than we did sex,
Our conversations became less stimulating
Inciting more outrage, than excitement in me
but nothing made me more certain that we were over than your inability
to make me smile like you once did.

My Substitute

I suppose I hurt you badly enough
For you to not want to see me again,
Seriously enough to block me.
But you made it a point
To post your new conquest,
Hoping I'd care,
And I don't,
Not one bit,
Knowing well
He's just a substitute
For what I can't give you.

On Being an Afterthought

It feels like I'm just an afterthought,
Someone you entertain out of necessity instead of love.

Some people are very good at convincing themselves they love us, but many people have yet to know what love is. For them, it is just a fancy foreign word they throw around to get what they want faster. Don't be afraid to love because of this, but do keep an eye open for what 'demands' are made after 'I Love You' or under what conditions it was said.

We've got to put an end to inconsistency.

Block off the people who continue claiming interest when it's only a fleeting sexual desire. But most important, it's time we say no to the person who wants to be with or spend time with us but is available only on his or her terms. That's not love. Love is an effortless continuation of desire to be with that special someone. It's about being there at two a.m. when the phone rings because you can't sleep. It's about going out of your way to show someone that she or he matters to you and you're there to support that person.

Let's stop allowing people to pencil us in like a doctor's appointment, because we deserve more, we deserve better. If you're in a relationship and don't feel like you can't count on them to be there for you, get out.

Option

I feel pathetic
Accepting this kind of love
Where you ignore me most days,
Choosing to respond at your will
When it's convenient, I suppose.
However so, I'm feeling less happy
About who I'm becoming,
Not knowing
If you'll ever truly love me.

About My Ex

You're worried about my ex,
Even though I've chosen you.
You wonder if there is still something there
Lingering, perhaps, from all our years together.
But I was a different person then.
I'm a new person now,
And I love only you.

On Imperfection

My mistake was focusing too much attention
On what wasn't happening instead of what was.
I never thought it would lead to our breakup.

Relationships aren't perfect, and neither are people. We run into problems when we're constantly pointing out our partner's faults or complaining about what they're not doing right.

How about shifting perspectives for a moment and acknowledging all the good things they are doing or the great qualities they have? We can't keep wanting a 'move-in ready' type of relationship, because they all require work and commitment to become the type of home we desire. Love who you're with for all that they are and yet to be.

Between Two

I'm still confused,
Unsure of which one of us you really want,
As if it should even be a question.
Shamefully, I don't recognize this new me,
Doubtful and insecure,
Unable to conquer my heart's desire
To stay and fight with uncertainty.

Bittersweet Promises

The smell of rotten love still lingers in the air,
That unmistakable fragrance of deception
Accompanied by notes of bittersweet promises
Of a better tomorrow,
Many of which I never got to see.

Residue

Residue from the mess
You created in my life
Remain splattered across walls I built
To keep you from climbing back in.
But you have a way
Of crawling into my heart—
Something like an insect
Looking to feed on me.

On Intuition

I'm with you,
And yet I feel so alone.

Often this is our soul speaking. We mustn't ignore it. We all try to establish relationships in which we have no business being, sometimes for the sake of having, and other times to cover up the fear of being alone. We can't plan love, no matter how strategic we get about it.

If and when you can, be with someone who asks about the details of your day and the dreams in your heart. Don't make the "choice" of settling for the sake of having. You're too wonderful for that.

TONIO

Pictures of us only remain
As live photos in my head,
And they play like a slideshow
Day in and day out,
Transitioning every second non-stop,
And sometimes I smile—
Even when it hurts.

An Unbearable Discomfort

I knew you were the one
The moment you made me promise
I wouldn't leave.
Your eyes, and the tone of your soul,
As they spoke the words,
Made me realize how much I meant to you
And that at last it was safe to settle down,
Because love couldn't be more demanding
Than in its plea to stay,
Because having to live without
Is an unbearable discomfort.

On Unrequited Love

Part of our lifelong journey is falling in love with someone who won't love us back the same. But that is not a direct reflection of our worth. It is just one of many valuable life lessons. Learn them well.

Every new chapter of our lives will require a different version of ourselves. We must remember that we're all on a journey for a different purpose. Some paths will cross, but it doesn't mean we're all going to the same destination. Don't take it personally when things don't work out with someone.

It will hurt, having to let go of everything you love—the sight of that person's beaming smile, the echoes of the voice that never seems to fade away—but we must remember that there are infinite emotions we've yet to experience outside the comforts of familiarity.

Finally, unrequited love holds a key lesson. For me it was reaching a place of total darkness where I fell, leaving me crippled, blind and emotionally disabled. I no longer mattered. And there was no one to remind me of how great I was once. Sadly, I became numb to all of the pain, as it had become a normal part of my existence, reaching out only to be turned away and humiliated.

Luckily enough, I had the courage one day to turn back to my faith, remembering that God doesn't judge us, and this too shall pass. I prayed many nights for the courage to walk away from it all, for the strength to open my eyes and finally see myself again.

And when I did, I knew I would never accept a situation like that ever again. I learned that anyone who is able to only receive and not ever give in return is someone who doesn't know the joys of love.

The Decision

I tried too hard to convince myself
That you were the one,
Neglecting my heart's desire
For someone better.
But now it's really time I go somewhere
Where I matter,
Not for what I can give,
But for all that I am.

On Hide and Seek

You tried to play a game of hide and seek
With my heart in the dark,
Kind of like when we were kids.
But we're not kids anymore,
And love isn't a game.
So I left you hiding alone in the dark.

When we're single, we'll likely meet a lot of these types of people who will string us along and leave us in the dark in terms of their feelings and intentions with us. Know that it's not us that's the problem, but sometimes it's all them—unsure of what they want or stand for. Be wise enough to know that courtship and 'chase,' as it's mostly called nowadays, are not the same.

If someone were to ever make you feel like a question mark when dating or in a relationship, please move on. Being unsure is a way of saying, "I'm not that into you."

It hurts deeply, having to feel like you're not good enough to be loved such as your heart desires. All I can say is, don't let that happen. Sometimes we'll be asked to wait until the other person is ready or when the time is perfect—in other words, while they continue to explore and test the waters.

Don't become an option for anyone. You're too valuable to be placed on hold, and vice versa. If ever we are hesitant to take that step with someone, it's not for nothing. Let that person go. Our soul, that part of us that knows best, is trying to tell us something. Don't ignore it.

On That Which Is Underneath Our Ugly

Most people will think they want you when you're attractive and looking your best. They'll assure and promise you that they want you when it's convenient. But remember, you won't always have perfect days, and when that time comes you'll want someone who can still see you underneath your ugly.

Never embark on a physical transformation journey so that someone can notice or love you. I guarantee you that person does not deserve your love. As well, you don't need that kind of conditional love.

I can't stress this enough. The person meant for you will see the real you behind layers of fat or any physical disfigurement. Whatever the case may be, we've got to stop pleasing a superficial society that continues to distort our real understanding of what Love is. They'll keep promoting a superficial kind of love for monetary gains and publicity. But do we ever stop to wonder how beautiful they all feel on the inside?

Whatever you decide to do with your body, do so because you want to, and you think it necessary for your personal growth. Not out of the pressure to please or attract artificial love. Out of the billions of people in the world, I assure you, there's a love promised for you. It may not always arrive when we want it to, but it does nevertheless.

On Rejection and Excuses

Most people give the excuse of working on themselves when in all honesty they're just not interested in us. It's time we become a little wiser and know the difference between excuses and truth. Many times, we hold back from telling one another the honest truth out of fear of hurting their feelings. But the truth of the matter is, we end up hurting them more when we string them along.

There are very few cases where someone may in all fairness not be ready to commit or give us the type of love we deserve. No matter how disappointing this may be, we should thank the person for honesty, because it takes courage to admit the truth. And that person deserves a paramount level of respect for bravery. We don't see much of this nowadays, as people find it easier to play games and keep as many options as possible open and on the sidelines than to risk someone not liking them.

And then there will be instances in which we are honest, and a person may not want to adhere, but will want to continue pursuing a false notion of love. But that's another topic for a different discussion.

People's emotions are real.
You cannot tell someone how to feel.
You may not understand it,
But you do have to respect it.

Opulence of Love

I'm not going to lie.
When I was with you, love was opulent.
I was spoiled from morning to night.
I had you in every way, every color.
And when we were away from each other,
I'd still feel your presence,
Because that was us then.
You gave me the luxury of love
Where nothing was ever to too much,
And I lost it all
To become a poor beggar
For someone else's attention
Whose love can never add up to yours.

Preview Trailer

I'll give you a movie trailer sample
Of what it's like inside my heart,
But don't mistake that for admission.
It takes a lot more than that
To become part of my story.

You tell me the most beautiful lies,
And I believe them all,
Because otherwise
You'd leave me in a brutal reality
Without you.

Her Saving Grace

My mom never knew true love. The man she loved always treated her like disposable income, spending her entire adult life at his mercy, never knowing what it was like to be saved until I came along. But her story still pains my soul, and the image of her lonely nights crying is still freshly painted in the back of my mind.

Isn't it crazy how you know
Exactly when your heart has been captured,
Stolen from you,
And yet you don't seek to recover it
Because you know it's in good hands?

My Alarm Clock

Mornings were definitely different
When you were around.
I never needed an alarm,
That was always your job,
Kissing my face until I woke.
You were always the more responsible one,
And now I must learn to be an adult.

Your Commitment

Every so often I'd make it a point
To remind you why I love you.
And though every day I find a new reason,
My favorite is still your commitment
To making me feel just as beautifully loved.

Starting Over

I'm not afraid of starting over.
Sometimes it's not always about them,
But more about the journey of self-discovery.
I welcome the unknown
And thank my past experiences
For all we shared, good and bad.

There is such a thing as a healthy obsession.
It's called LOVE.

Missing You

When I miss you,
I become deaf to the world around me.
Tuning in to the sound of my heart
Playing our favorite song
As it brings you closer to a place
More perfect than any dream
Where my every desire
Of having you close
Is fulfilled.

Loved and Lost

Truth is, I've been hurt before.
I've loved, then lost,
But I lie and say it's never happened,
Love has not yet found me,
When in actuality I've loved.
I guess it's easier to avoid
Having to explain the details
Of why we didn't make it.

On Egotism

When we're unaware of ourselves, we tend to blame all of our lack of love on others. It's always them, not us, needing change. Yet we have to take full responsibility and ownership of our lives.

It's normal to think that love doesn't come easy—and it doesn't for those of us, stuck in our bad habits, too stubborn to rectify or compromise. We live in an egotistical society now, and that's the sad reality, but until we make that effort to humble ourselves and understand that we're not perfect and nobody owes us anything, we'll always take steps back in every relationship with each other. If love is what we're seeking, then we must be that love we want to attract.

Responsibilities

I know you're hurting for me,
Crying because of me,
But it was never my intention
To make you happy longer
Than in that moment of pleasure.
I've never been the type to stay longer
Than the time it takes
To make you believe in love
Until I run scared of responsibilities.

It never gets old.
Every morning I stare at you in disbelief,
Unable to make sense
Of how in the world you're mine.

Undress my heart.
Expose the nudity of my love
As only you can.
Take off all the pride and fear covering it up
So I can know vulnerability.
So I can know you.

Tonight

Tonight you're sleeping in my arms,
Nestled in my warm embrace
Because you're my saving grace.
I love you without a doubt,
And I won't close my eyes
Until I know you feel safe to love again.

A Naked Heart

Most people praying for love
Have no idea what it is,
And when blessed with love,
They dismiss it because
It doesn't look like what they envisioned.
But love is not seen with the naked eye—
Instead, with a naked heart.

Making Love

You're annoying.
You don't ever allow me to sleep.
And when I finally do,
That's when you kiss me just the way I like.
And then it happens again,
Because I never wait to make love to you.

On Love as an Adhesive

Titles don't hold relationships together.
LOVE does.

Sometimes, just because we're in a relationship or marriage, we think we have it all; once we've got the title of 'boyfriend,' 'girlfriend,' 'husband' or 'wife,' we're all set. But we forget that, unless we have someone's heart and absolute love, we have absolutely nothing. Love is the only adhesive that can keep a healthy relationship together. It's time we stop striving for the title and start reaching for the heart. I can't stress enough how many times I hear people bragging about how many sexual conquests they've had while in a relationship or married. It baffles me, the level of disrespect, and, no, you don't get cool points for cheating on your husband or wife!

Take it for what it is.
Love in the moment.
Don't overthink it,
Anticipating forever.
Allow time to take you there.

Beyond the Cover Page

You're the first to see
The fear in my heart,
The first to solve the mystery
Hidden in my eyes,
And I love you for reading me
Beyond the cover page.

The Magic of Love

You and I are magicians
In our own right.
Without trickery, we create
This magical moment of love
Every time we touch.

I overheard you practicing
For the perfect delivery
Of your first 'I love you,'
But nothing said it best
Than that kiss.

A Moment Closer

You have no idea what it's like
Waking up with you in mind,
Feeling dreamlike,
So I'm always behind schedule
Rushing through the day,
Hoping every second passing
Is a moment closer to the time
When I'll see you.

The Melodies of Love

Like the melodies of love,
That song you sing
Always takes me to a happy place
Where I'm yours and you're mine,
Feeling ever so perfect
In how we feel,
In how we love.

It's incredible.
We could be anywhere
Doing absolutely nothing,
And it could still feel
Like the best time of our lives.

On Evaluating Love

People will love us the way they know how. It's up to us to decide if their kind of love is what's best for our soul.

Not all love is the same, just as not all 'love' is good love. People will proclaim an undying love for us, but if that love doesn't make our soul soar, it honestly isn't meant for us. We shouldn't get into a relationship or, in most cases today, a "situationship" just because someone says 'I love you.' The type of love intended for us will transcend beyond this reality and time. Any relationship we get into should add and not take away from us. The best kind of love allows us to mature and grow in ways we never thought possible. No two persons will ever love us the same, so we must stop comparing our exes with our current partners, and vice versa. Otherwise, we would never experience all of the depths and heights of love.

On Love and Trust

I feel as though I can't trust anyone with my heart, so the only way I'll ever lose it would be through an elaborate romantic heist.

We cannot blindly trust anyone these days. We may know someone our entire life, and in a moment's time they turn their backs on us. The same goes for modern-day relationships and friendships: too many of us give our hearts away easily without making sure the other person even wants it. And we entrust that person with the most beautiful parts of us, only to make us feel worthless in return, because, when we keep giving something so valuable like love, we end up feeling depreciated.

Remember, we live in different times, in which everything we could possibly want is available with the snap of a finger. A lot of people are walking around with no moral compass, and they don't care who's married or who's in a loving relationship; they will make every attempt to intrude, take what they want, and destroy your home.

Take the time to know someone on every level possible. Avoid sexual manipulation, and build an honest friendship. I understand the human need for sexual gratification—and most times we find a way to execute our lack of self control on our animalistic instincts—but, until we do things differently, we will always get the same results: finding someone new to sleep with, and once that's no longer fun, we move on to the next, in search of 'love,' except most people have yet to develop the courage or knowledge to know and understand that love is ultimately what they seek.

On Romance

I miss the excitement of new romance,
The anxiousness of seeing you again,
The willingness to go the distance,
But somehow we've made the mistake
Of complacency.

"Complacency: A feeling of being satisfied with the way things are and not wanting to make them better."

To keep love alive and your relationship blossoming, water it with romance. Do kind things for one another spontaneously—and it doesn't require spending money on gifts for one another. Perhaps you open the car door if you don't already do so. If you don't currently live together, show up unannounced with breakfast or dinner. Write each other love notes…

We often mistake lack of passion for lack of love. Some of us even confuse the two, thinking they mean the same. Passion is a strong desire or emotion, almost like a fuel that keeps love burning. It's the excitement we get when love is in its infancy stage. However, sometimes routine and life can get in the way of once-beautiful relationships. This is why it's important that we romance each other, flirt as we did before getting into the relationship, try new things, explore the yet conquered territories of each other's heart, because love goes beyond the titles of 'boyfriend,' 'girlfriend,' 'wife' and 'husband.' Just because we got with the person of our dreams doesn't mean we should stop giving them attention or being detailed. It's easy to allow life and outside stressors get in the way, but it's important that we make time and prioritize our relationship so that we continue to add fuel to the fire. As long as there is love, there's hope it can be saved.

Spontaneity is a great way to keep the suspense going in a relationship. It is also one of the best ways to keep a relationship interesting, alive, and exciting. We shouldn't get comfortable thinking that, once we get with the person we wanted, we ought to stop doing what we did to get them. I recommend we continue to flirt with each other, never stop exploring each other's heart, always embark on new emotional journeys, take weekend trips whenever possible, and have unplanned dinner dates.

We must never get into the habit of doing the bare minimum or what is expected just to get along. In love, we should always go the distance and exceed each other's expectations. After all, isn't love limitless?

I just pray tomorrow things change.
Hopefully I'll love you differently
And think of you less.
Enough to give me a chance
To escape this cycle of abuse.

You feel like a daydream…
A world of infinite possibilities
Detached from a present moment
Of uncertain reality.

Morning Magic

I know my life would be so much better
If I could just wake up
Next to you every morning,
But that's not our storyline yet.
So I'll keep waiting until you realize
He's not the one
And then we can start something
Truly magical.

Pain of Absence

Your last voice message,
Pictures of you,
And photographs of us
Are all that remain,
Accompanied by a lingering pain of absence
That never seems to go away.
And I remember you just as you were,
That last time I saw you smiling
As if nothing bothered you.
I swear I knew every blemish and wrinkle
On your face.
I loved looking at you
More than I did
Our once-upon-a-time favorite TV show.
God knows I hate you
For leaving me so soon,
Even though you promised me
Your heart is mine forever—
But I just wish you were still here
To fight with me,
Because no one else is worth the fight,
And, knowing you,
I'm sure you're looking down at me smiling,
Because my love is always guaranteed to you.

And when I'm not thinking of you,
I'm dreaming of you.
There's no end to this crazy,
Sexy obsession with you.

Remain cognizant that most people only love the idea of you. The moment you reveal a flaw contradictory to their idyllic perception of you, love ceases to exist.

Off Road

I didn't think we'd be veering off road
So soon after you promised eternity.
I didn't know I was bad company
On a journey I figured we were in together.
But you never really spoke your mind,
And now I'm walking alone on deserted territory
Trying to find the road where we first met,
But, of course, I can't remember.
I never was aware how absent I'd become
Until it was too late.

On the Truth About Love

There is in fact no end to love. And sometimes, for whatever reason, we are forced to separate from someone we love wholeheartedly, and other times, obliged to love that someone differently. Yet true love never dies. Separations are just other steps in our journey to love. No love story is ever written to perfection, because it simply does not exist, and we need the kind of love that is volatile and imperfectly honest. Regardless of the outcome, we must be glad love happened to us, because it is a blessing to love someone and be loved in return.

I am blessed to have discovered love in a way that is imperfect but genuine, never seeking to put me down in any way. And I must say, I've learned that people will love you differently, sometimes not exactly the way we anticipated love to be. But it's not our place to discredit their love, because in all actuality those who will love us best have no script to read, nor have they rehearsed how to act out love.

And to you...who makes 'Us' a never-ending love story, 'I love you' is simply not enough at this point to begin explaining how extraordinarily amazing I feel every time I look at you. And I know that you know—I adore you and will always enter that battlefield ready to fight, conquer and win your heart—however many times I need to—so we can make it to eternity.

On Cheating

It will happen to the best of us. Someone we vowed to love or commit to will dishonor and betray us in the most horrific way. They'll choose to lay with another for whatever reason, and when we find out, it will hurt. It will crush our hearts. But here's the thing: although it will hurt, it won't kill us.

Forgiveness will at first seem unreasonable. But it will be necessary for our healing. We will have a million questions that will forever go unanswered, and then we'll begin to question ourselves and our self-worth, as if we had a part in it or we're to blame. But whatever happens, we must remember that we're not the first or last person this will happen to.

Cry if we must. Take a moment to sulk and be upset and angry about it all. But the minute we're done, get back up and start again. Start a new and better relationship with ourselves. Bad things happen to good people all the time, and what defines them is, how well they rise up from it all.

I can give us a million reasons why we shouldn't cheat on someone who loves us, but none of them will stop it from happening if we are so inclined. At the end of the day, the only person we're cheating is ourselves.

There will come a day when you'll wish you still had that person who gave it all to you without exceptions. For there's nothing more horrifying than trying to imagine your life without someone you love, no matter how angry or upset we may be. Yet genuine love is real but rare. When we find it, it's up to us to do all we can to keep that love alive and growing.

Things won't always be perfect in a relationship, but it doesn't mean it won't work or that it's time for a breakup. And, quite honestly, the people who turn to a breakup as the first option were never meant for you in the first place. I know by now you're probably saying to yourself that I'm contradicting myself, but no. Once someone cheats, that's it. They are gone from my life. I may forgive, but I'll never forget, nor will I ever give that person a warm welcome back.

And here's where the problem lies: We've become accustomed to certain behaviors and have normalized many things that shouldn't be. Cheating has become one of them. And every time someone takes back a cheater who dishonored their love, we're contributing to that false sense of normalcy.

This may be a bold statement but accepting someone back into your life who's done that to you is a form of disrespect. I'll stand by this for as long as I live. And perhaps I don't know any better yet. But my heart is my most precious gift, and I won't allow anyone to disrespect me in such a blatant way. It's not as though cheating is a mistake or an accident. People have choices and options.

All I can hope is that people will treat us in the manner we allow them to. By our actions in taking someone back after they've betrayed our trust and our love, we're sending the message that cheating is OK.

And look—no matter what you're going through or how bad everything seems right now in your life, never forget that you're important and beautiful. Don't ever let anyone make you feel or think otherwise. I know so, because I am you. We are all the same in that we feel pain.

Cheating on someone you're with is no mistake. It's a choice—one that often has grave consequences and long-lasting effects on the victim. The other person is a victim because they give their heart and love to an unsuspecting person whom they trust, only to be defrauded and hurt because they don't understand loyalty and fidelity.

I understand the current society we live in. I am aware of the multitude of hungry serpents who dare try to take a bite out forbidden love, to invade the personal space of a loving relationship because they can't stand to see others happy, or simply out of pure desperation to satisfy they carnal appetite.

Temptation lurks—online and in person everywhere you go—but that's never an excuse for going outside of your marriage or relationship. Betraying someone who loves and trusts you is a crime in the court of love. And though at first it may hurt the person you cheated on, someday you'll realize regrettably how stupid and childish the act is.

If you know you can't commit, be honest about it.

"I don't suppose you know the pain you caused, or how much it all still hurts, despite the number of times you've said you're sorry. Guess you never stopped to think how your betrayal would affect me the moment you chose to lie down with another."

Here's the truth of the matter: *Cheating is wrong.*

If you're with someone and know you cannot trust or control yourself to remain faithful, be honest about it and end the relationship. Don't take the cowardly route and cheat on that person just because you don't have the courage to break things off. If you're honest, you'll get more respect in the end for being honest with yourself, your feelings, and your significant others. The effects of betrayal, on the other hand, are long-lasting, and, no matter how many times you apologize, it still doesn't fix the hurt. It's something that those who have truly loved you will carry with them wherever they go.

Whatever the situation may be, however lonely or perhaps angry you may be, there is never a justification for cheating. Emotional betrayal leaves an ugly scar on someone's heart. And sometimes the wound is so deep and severe it makes it difficult for one to trust and love again.

P.T.R.D.

(Post-Traumatic Relationship Disorder)

Somehow it all remains
Vivid despite time.
Present in every moment,
Regardless of how far I've come.
Torturous memories, invaders
Who now inhabit my mind—
Remind me of how it used to be.
And my body, dressed in fear,
Seeks pleasure in strangers to no avail,
Since my mind is numb,
And my body doesn't react
To anyone who is not you.
I wonder still
In the silence of my lonely heart,
Thinking, 'Why?'
Feeling less than small,
Unfit to stand beside anyone else,
Afraid it will happen again,
Frightened that they, too, will betray me
Because I'm to blame.
I'm too lame.
I can no longer tell the truth from a lie,
So I don't believe a thing,
And all smiles

Are untrustworthy and deceptive
Like the one that stole my heart.

Everything Remains the Same

I still find strands of your hair
In places we used to lay.
I smile and wonder if you still think of me
Just as much as I think of you,
Because I haven't changed a thing.
Everything remains the same
If ever you decide to come back home.

The Champion

You're the MVP of my heart,
Winning it over and over again
Like a championship,
Knowing how to swiftly
Maneuver your way around
In a place that is all yours.

Beyond Words

You're the most amazing person I know.
I love you with all my strength
And all of my heart.
There isn't a thing I wouldn't do
Or a place I wouldn't go
For you.
Every day you teach me more
About love and life.
You inspire my soul to keep soaring,
And for that, I am forever yours,
Beyond words,
Beyond this lifetime.

The Doors of My Heart

I can't remember
The last time I felt like this
After a kiss.
Utterly speechless,
Suspended in a moment of complete silence
Where the absence of fear was obvious
And I could feel the doors of my heart
Finally open
Just enough for you to sneak in.

The Eighth Wonder

I'm excited to kiss new lips,
Get lost in new eyes,
Conquer the territories of your heart
And allow my hands to travel freely
Around the eighth wonder of this world—
Your body.

Every Thought of You

There's just no way of denying such love,
Whereby, no matter how astutely
I attempt to hide it,
I just can't seem to catch all the times
My heart escapes my chest and jumps at you.
And my smile—I don't know where to begin,
But it's effortless and infinite
To the point where the muscles tire
With the desire
To keep on smiling every time you are near,
Or simply with every thought of you.

A Place Beyond

I keep falling in love with you.
Every kiss is a new experience,
Every touch is an incredible journey
To a place beyond,
And your smile continues being
A must-see production.

Perseverance

I will show you just how beautiful life is,
Because we chose love in each other.
I intend to touch your heart
Every unexpected moment,
Regardless of how many times
You get angry with me.
And, most important,
I am going to fight for us
In every battle and world war.

My Appetite for You

I am a hopeful romantic
Filled to the brim with sweet love.
My desire is rich and intensely decadent.
I crave the moments and kisses
That satisfy my appetite for you.

A Dream

You remind me of a dream I once had,
Vividly enchanting,
Unbelievably magical,
And amazingly beautiful.
I keep seeing you,
And I ponder the possibility
Of someday having the courage enough
To approach you
And perhaps share with you
The dream of us in love.

Waking Up

You follow me into every dream.
Day or night, you're always there,
Waiting our encounter,
But nothing compares to the dream
That is waking up to your face,
Knowing time after time
That you are mine
And I am yours.

'It's Okay'

I still remember the day
You walked into my life
And slowly undressed my heart.
I watched as you whispered, 'It's okay,'
Assuring me you weren't like the others
While fearlessly caressing the once rough surfaces.
Today, I've got a beautifully naked heart
With your lips tattooed all over.

My dearest love
How can I ever begin to thank you for all the amazing ways you've made me feel
in the little time I've known you?
How do I ask you to spend an eternity with me because I've never been so sure of
anyone else or anything the way I am about us?

On Worthiness

Sometimes in life we fall in love with people who aren't used to being loved the way we love. It will hurt, because we love so profoundly and intensely, and no matter what we do to show this love, they'll never see it, they'll never understand it. Regardless of their reception of our love, we should never for a second begin to wonder whether or not we are enough—because we are. We always will be more than enough—just not to them.

I truly hope this will serve as a reminder for any of you who may be questioning your worth at this very moment. No matter who you are or where life has taken you, you are still worthy of love. You're amazing beyond anyone's perception or opinion of you. Your love is a valued gift to someone who is destined for you, remember that.

A Magic of Love

It's unbelievable
How much I love you.
Catching myself smiling
At just how beautiful this all feels—
To be in love,
To be yours,
And you mine.
It all feels like a dream,
But you remind me every moment that,
Yes, we're like characters in a fairytale,
But this story of us
Is all a magic of love.

On Finding the 'Right One'

I remember
Every note I've ever written to you,
Every restaurant we've ever been to,
And every moment I have fallen in love with you.

We tend to naturally remember the important dates and moments that define us. Falling in love is one of them. We blossom into an even more beautiful being when we're in love, possessing extraordinary abilities and superhuman strength. This is part of why we say, "A person's heart will never forget how you make them feel."

And this is why we ought to treat one another kindly and specially every chance we get. Sometimes just a single moment of our time is all that's needed to help someone through a difficult time. It's all an act of love.

We don't just fall in love one time with the same person. When we find the 'right one,' it's a complete new experience every time we're with that one. Everything we do will be amplified, and we'll always feel like there are more territories to that special someone's heart in need of our exploration.

I want you in every way imaginable,
Just as you are.
And I swear I've never seen anyone
As perfect as you are for me.

On the Wrong Person

So many people are coming and going home
To the wrong person at this very moment.
They'll never admit or end it
Because familiarity is safe.
It's comfortable.

Perhaps it's our upbringing, lack of self-love, or fear of being alone. Whatever the reason, many of us are holding on to the wrong person. We're lying to ourselves but can't fool our hearts—so much that we've forgotten what love is really like. And that it's supposed to make us feel alive. It's supposed to inspire us to grow and be our best selves. Instead, we choose to play pretend and build a home out of gratitude and fear instead of love and honesty.

This piece isn't about judgment, but more of an attempt to provide an honest look at how things are. This is why no one should try to imitate another person's idea or image of 'happiness.' Not every happy home is a happy home, and not every smile is real. Love exists, and we can all discover it the moment we begin to have an honest heart-to-heart conversation with ourselves.

On Timing

Soulmates don't find each other.
They meet as destined.

I know that many people are worried thinking they are running out of time when it comes to finding love. So often they rush into something with whoever is available.

But what point is there in 'finding love' if you're going to be unhappy or with someone who's not in love with you? Focus on yourself and be the best person you can be. Love will arrive as destined.

Look at all of the wonderful people in your life who just showed up and found their special place in your heart. Do you think it was all by accident? Of course not! The same goes for romantic love—when it's your timing, it will happen.

I hate that a simple thought of you excites me.
And your voice makes me forget
Why I'm mad at you in the first place.

I've always thought I was able-bodied
Until I couldn't walk away from you.

On Transformation

You seduce and undress my insecurities
With a powerful gaze,
And I'm amazed
By what love looks like in your eyes.

It can be at times the most terrifying thing to do: stare into someone's eyes. But when we do, there's just something so magical and magnificent that transpires…like falling in love, for instance. Sometimes when we're in love, we are transformed. We become better people, better friends. The right person by our side gives us a different perspective. That person allows us to see ourselves differently from a different vantage point—not by criticizing or belittling us, but by simply loving us regardless of…and we fill in the rest.

Love is inspiring at best. Don't ever allow someone to start loving you only when you're at 'your best.' It shouldn't take a major weight loss or physical transformation for someone to magically fall for you. That is mere attraction—a conditional form of 'love' that will last just as long as your looks don't fade.

On Continuing the Love

You still have to flirt with each other after the 'I do.'

Sometimes the problem lies in that we stop putting in the effort. We stop doing the things we did to get the person we love. Perhaps some of us feel that marriage or a relationship is the ultimate destination so once we get the title of husband, wife, boyfriend or girlfriend, we are set. We stop trying. But that's the mistake so many of us make. We still have to make each other feel as though we are the only boy or girl in the world.

Disturb Me

Relationships today are so weird. Two people who supposedly love one another and yet will go days without speaking or seeing each other. Perhaps I failed to change with the times, because I'd never settle for that nonsense.

I don't know about you, but I don't want to be with someone who makes excuses for why they haven't called or texted in hours or days. In life, I find that the person who isn't afraid to 'disturb' us at work is the person we need to get to know.

The truth is, we all know that someone who really wants to talk with us or see us will find a way. People can give us all of the excuses in the world, but it's up to us whether or not we stay around to continue listening. What else could be more exciting than showing that new love potential you're interested by sneaking off to the work bathroom, making that 30-second phone call, and reminding that person that she or he is on your mind? I say all this to say that, there's always a way. I know that when I'm in love with you, you'll never have to question it.

Oh, and one more thing. Love doesn't set schedules for when one person should be available for the other. We should never feel as though we are being restricted access when it comes to communicating with our lover.

The Afterthought

I allowed you to make me feel
Like an afterthought,
And that's my fault.
I knew all along
There were two of us
You needed to keep happy, and
Although you swear
I'm the one you love,
I cannot accept
This kind of relationship.
It tears my heart in half
Having to walk away from you,
But I trust that somewhere out there
Is someone for me
Who will not hesitate to make me
Their first choice
And only choice.

On Knowing When to Let Go

Like most people, I thought I had found the one. More than willing, I was ready to take every next step necessary so we could be happy together. But, unbeknownst to me, someone else was already in the position I had hoped to have in your life. And perhaps I didn't ask all of the right questions from the beginning, or, quite honestly, I ignored the signs, the inconsistency in your stories, and the fact that you never could make that commitment to me. That is why I am here in this, a final chapter in the story of us, because, although I love you, I've got to love myself a little more, just enough to choose what's best for me, and that's not you.

My friends, I would have wished that this story would have had a conventional type of happy ending—where we run off into the sunset, perhaps, and to some it may not be—while for me it is a happy ending. It has been an interesting chapter of uncovering my self-worth and self-discovery. For that I am grateful, to you who broke my heart many times over, and to you who didn't know how to value me such that you wanted to keep me. This has been but a tremendous life lesson, that in many ways I owe to you.

I was able to make a heartbreaking decision, but ultimately a good one, because now I can move on and allow my heart to heal, and most of all, continue on that special journey to love. I know that my story is not yet over, and that forever is that place and time I hope to visit someday with someone who'll always know with certainty that with me is where they'd rather be.

Understand that I'm not bitter—I'm *better* because of you, and I forgive you for all of the sleepless nights and teary eyes. I thank you for the wonderful moments we had, because I'd be lying if I said otherwise. I still think you're something wonderful, or else I wouldn't have loved you the way I did— but I know now you're just not the one for me.

As for me, I know I'll be OK—because there's a peace in my heart I haven't felt in a very long time, and that's because I'm not worrying about whether or not someone I love is out there being unfaithful or whether they're telling me the truth. I'm glad I came to the realization that certain kinds of love are toxic and not worthwhile if I have to constantly worry instead of growing.

A lot of times we lose sleep and our peace of mind worrying about someone who's ultimately not ours to keep. We have to begin to understand that the one meant for us—will do whatever it takes to make sure we smile every day and that their love for us is never in question. Anyone else —who behaves such that it creates doubt in our hearts; should be let go.

We cannot be afraid to ask ourselves all of the uncomfortable questions, fearful the answers will hurt or cause us discomfort, because when we don't, we allow others to think for us, and then we settle.

Love,
You'll never die.
I've written you such that
The world may never know your name,
But you'll live forever
In the hearts of all
Who read the story of us.

Final Thoughts

A Book About Us: A Heart's Continuing Journey to Love was by far one of the hardest most heartbreaking chapters to write and also a significant one. It took me on an emotional journey back to a dark past I thought I had forgotten: *my childhood*. There, I was forced to come face to face with the young version of myself in one final attempt to treat and help heal my wounds from the past.

I wasn't sure at first why the sudden transportation to that exact point and time, but it soon became very clear why. It was all a reminder of how far I'd come and why I started writing in the first place. And that was because when I couldn't communicate my pain and suffering to the adults in my life, the notebooks, initially meant for note taking in class became my friends. They became my allies and confidants to whom I would pour all of my hurt and emotions. Many of which I did with tear-filled eyes, now that I recall.

Growing up my family wasn't exactly the kind that expressed a lot of love or affection. Culturally it was the norm and children were taught to be tough, and we wouldn't ever see a therapist because that's for "crazy people." You get the idea. As a result, I subconsciously distanced myself from self-expression. I did what I was told, pleased who I needed to please and allowed everyone else to make decisions for me. I ultimately in the process forgot how to think and feel for myself.

I shied away from showing emotions most times or reacted nonchalantly to matters of love. Long into my adult life, I would dismiss anyone who professed their love for me. Reducing their feelings and emotions to mere lust. Or at times I'd find reasons to make them hate me and run away. In a sense, I suppose I was afraid of love.

I don't wish to blame or fault anyone for my mistakes except myself. Frankly, a lot of the sadness and emptiness I have experienced has allowed me to write incredible pieces of puzzles yet to be completed.

Every bit of pain and suffering I've had to endure, has brought me here, to this very paragraph at the end of this book about *us*. Us as humans and the different ways we love and cope. Us as the union between two people who love each other. In theory, I've become an explicit writer of the human emotion, an author of love for the brokenhearted. In this way, I measure most of my success—success at touching hearts with words so that it allows a person's heart to begin to heal wounds of love from the inside-out.

Life is strange at times. I've woken up many mornings to a stranger in the mirror looking back at me, not knowing how multidimensional people are. I was blind to the complexity of human emotions or how sporadic and unreasonable we can be. In this sense, I realized I couldn't honestly understand love if all I thought of was myself. And it's easy to forget to place ourselves in the other person's shoes because we're taught to be selfish—it's all about 'I,' the single pronoun—until the selfish behavior keeps ruining our relationships with potentially good people.
Regardless of what has transpired over the years, I've maintained a ravenous appetite for love—and not just any kind. Because 'modern love,' as it is commonly termed, is all but a superficial idea of what we as a society have reshaped love to be. And, as all of you may have witnessed, it never quite lasts longer than months, if not weeks, at a time.

This happens for several reasons, but one primary reason is that people are getting into relationships without the strongest, most unbinding adhesive—love. No wonder bonds aren't formed, and we walk out on one another as if nothing happened, because, in actuality, nothing did happen. It was a superficial attempt at conquering love, driven by a fleshly desire.

Enough about the why—if you've journeyed this far with me, thank you. I hope *A Book About Us* brings you a step closer to your journey to love. And if you've already found your 'once in a lifetime,' congratulations on such great achievement, because, as you'll soon see, love is a never-ending battle fought among those ready to win it all.

In closing, it was important to write this book from a place of honesty. To do so, I had to allow my heart to bleed freely into the pages. I hope it was evident to you that my heart has been cut and torn into pieces like scrap paper—but remains resilient and beautifully written.

www.ingramcontent.com/pod-product-compliance
Lightning Source LLC
Chambersburg PA
CBHW021927040426
42448CB00008B/942